It is good to have plants which literally smile back at you.

FRED REICHEL
secretary to Warden James Johnston (1934–1941)

Shirley poppy
Papaver rhoeas

Alcatraz Gardens

REMEMBERED, RECLAIMED, REIMAGINED

Introduction by Susan Heeger

Photographs by
Elizabeth Byers and Shelagh Fritz

THE GARDEN CONSERVANCY
GOLDEN GATE NATIONAL PARKS CONSERVANCY
San Francisco, California

Golden Gate National Parks Conservancy
Bldg. 201, Fort Mason
San Francisco, CA 94123
www.parksconservancy.org

ISBN 978-1-932519-30-3

Library of Congress Control Number: 2013934457

Cover Photo: Alison Taggart-Barone
Project Coordinator: Elizabeth Byers
Design: Vivian Young
Editor: Susan Tasaki
Production: Sarah Lau Levitt

Developed and designed in the US

In 1996, the Golden Gate National Parks Conservancy published Gardens of Alcatraz *(Introduction by Delphine Hirasuna; essays by John Hart, Russell A. Beatty, and Michael Boland; photographs by Roy Eisenhardt). The book, which documented the remarkable variety of plant life on the island and placed it in historical and cultural context, raised awareness of the gardens' value to those who lived on Alcatraz, and brought attention to the need to preserve the gardens before they were lost forever.*

Printed in Hong Kong

Dahlia 'Kaiser Wilhelm'

If we are all our own jailers and prisoners of our traits, then I am grateful for my introduction to the spade and the trowel, the seed and the spray can. They have given me a lasting interest in creativity.

ELLIOTT MICHENER
Inmate number AZ-578 (1941-1950)

Preface
The Alcatraz Historic Gardens Project

*F*rom the mid-nineteenth century until the closure of the federal prison in 1963, the gardens on Alcatraz brought an air of civility to the island's residents, and became places of refuge for inmates. But when the island opened to the public in 1973, no visual evidence of these historic gardens or sense of their history remained.

The overgrown gardens were neglected until 2003, when, in collaboration with the National Park Service, the Garden Conservancy and the Golden Gate National Parks Conservancy began to bring the gardens of Alcatraz back to life. With the help of enthusiastic groups of volunteers, dedicated staff, and generous foundation and agency funders, the first stewardship program for cultural resources was created.

The challenge was daunting. After an intensive year of removing decades of accumulated plant debris, the team discovered that many of the garden's historical structural features—terraces, paths, railings, and foundations—were still in place but needed repair. Plants that had been buried began to flourish after removal of invasive species. Even small-scale features such as stepping-stones and inmate graffiti reappeared.

In 2005, after studying historic photos, plans, maps, and oral histories, the project partners began preparing detailed rehabilitation plans for five garden areas. Photographs, mostly from the penitentiary era, helped determine those plantings that would provide the appropriate look and feel of the historic gardens. Over a four-year period, staff and volunteers repaired structures, stabilized slopes, and replanted the five gardens with both legacy and newly introduced plants.

The garden project is a model of sustainability, with a water catchment system used for irrigation, a composting system that recycles the gardens' biomass, and a palette of drought-tolerant plants. The rainwater catchment system, rehabilitated from historical cisterns that had captured gray water from the prison's showers, holds 12,000 gallons, enough to keep all the island's gardens healthy year round.

Today, visitors strolling through the blooming gardens reap the rewards of many years of planning and rebuilding. The gardens' interpretive program ensures that the thousands of people who visit the island every day are able to appreciate the gardens as an important part of our cultural heritage. Docent tours are offered, a self-guiding brochure is

available, eight waysides provide historical inform-
ation, and a website *(alcatrazgardens.org)* is dedicated to
the project.

Proceeds from the sale of this book will help
provide funding for the gardens. Thank you for
your support.

—Elizabeth Byers
Preservation Projects Consultant
The Garden Conservancy

Pelargonium 'Mrs. Langtry'

Narcissus 'Grand Soleil d'Or'

Introduction

RECLAIMING THE ROCK

During the short ferry ride from San Francisco to Alcatraz, visitors to the island are likely to notice an eerie transformation. The closer the boat gets to this former military-fortification-turned-prison outpost, the more the cellhouse and other structures—tall and forbidding at a distance—seem to crumble.

Trees spread their sheltering boughs over paths and steps, framing peaceful water views. Blooming vines clamber up stout stone walls, some only ruins against the sky. Gulls stalk the rubble of a military parade ground wreathed in century plants.

As the boat slows, turns, and chugs toward the dock, a softer, greener world overwhelms the message of confinement, illuminating the island's paradox: even on wave-washed, isolated Alcatraz, people have planted gardens, and the gardens, to some small or large degree, set them free.

Wandering through these gardens today, newly restored by the Garden Conservancy and the Golden Gate National Parks Conservancy, brings the paradox alive. In contrast to the desolation of the prison—each cell a concrete vault for a man—the

Above and below: Citadel garden, circa 1870.

plants are vivid and persistent, thriving with the passing years.

California poppies and coyote brush have grown here since the late nineteenth century, when they sprouted from soil barged to Alcatraz from nearby Angel Island. Roses and iris mark spots where Victorian-era army wives, transferred here with their husbands, tried to civilize what was then a defensive post for San Francisco, and later, a military lock-up. Cypress and eucalyptus have endured from the 1920s, when the California Spring Blossom and Wild Flower Association assumed the task of beautifying the barren island. After Alcatraz became a super-max penitentiary for America's worst criminals in the early 1930s, the Pride of Madeira's purple flower spikes showed up.

Each era, each wave of habitation, brought gardens developed for different reasons. Victorian wives longed for the refinements of home; the plant society (we might imagine) had a sleeves-rolled-up urge to do good. The convict gardeners, exiled by an indifferent world, sought relief in coaxing green from the cold inertia of "the Rock."

It wasn't easy. Ripped by winds and wreathed in fog, Alcatraz had no resources of its own. Soil,

water, plants—everything that makes a landscape—
had to be ferried here, often at great expense. Yet
successive generations, inspired by what earlier
gardeners had done, continued to seed and nurture
plants.

One such newcomer was the prison warden's
secretary, Fred Reichel. Surprised and moved by the
bits of "intensely interesting" landscape he found
when he took up his post, he resolved to develop
more, to further ease the island's bleakness. For
help building flowerbeds and terracing slopes, he
enlisted a hand-picked, hard-bitten crew, which
included convicted counterfeiter Elliott Michener.

Michener began his new outdoor assignment
plotting escape but fell in love with the work, and
kept at it seven days a week until he left Alcatraz
in 1950. A novice gardener, he learned from seed
packets, constructed a greenhouse from building
scraps, and hybridized his own narcissus. Before
long, his fellow inmates had blooming borders to
enjoy as they marched to their jobs on the prison
grounds. More than a few snatched flowers for their
cells from the brilliant living carpets that could be
seen from San Francisco.

After the prison closed in 1963, the landscape
languished amid debate over what to do with the

Inmate in Officers' Row garden, circa 1940s.

*I kept no records of my failures, for I had many—
the main thing was to assure some success by trying
many things and holding on to those plants which
had learned that life is worth holding onto even at
its bitterest.*

FRED REICHEL
secretary to Warden James Johnston (1934-1941)

Prison employees and their families enjoyed the gardens as well; Officers' Row, 1961.

The gardens of Alcatraz are testaments to the human spirit, to the desire to create life and beauty even in a forbidding environment. Perhaps this above all is what makes them so inspiring— and so touching.

DELPHINE HIRASUNA
Gardens of Alcatraz

island. Eventually, in 1972, Alcatraz was folded into the then brand-new Golden Gate National Recreation Area, a unit of the National Park Service. Today, around its remaining buildings, the gardens grow and bloom, living layers of its history.

Their restoration was part of a Herculean effort begun in 2003 when, after years of neglect, many had withered to nothing, or surged into jungles that buried walls and swallowed walks.

In certain places, where time had erased the evidence, the renovations were reimaginings rather than literal recreations. In others, volunteers combing through the thickets uncovered treasures from forgotten times: the Victorians' roses, callas, and fuchsias, the convict-planted figs. All, in their way, are enduring symbols of the gardeners' hopes and determination: to scratch something out of meagerness, confound expectations, and defy the odds by wringing beauty from a bitter rock.

—Susan Heeger

Rosa 'Gruss an Achen'

When we realize the extraordinary effort that was required to create that beauty, aesthetic appreciation becomes visceral. Suddenly, we appreciate the true meaning of the gardens: the human drama they represent. They are transformed from simple, lovely artifacts of the past to part of a dynamic process that changed the lives of the gardeners, who invested not only their energies but also their spirits.

RUSSELL A. BEATTY
Gardens of Alcatraz

You become responsible, forever,
for what you have tamed.

ANTOINE DE SAINT-EXUPÉRY
The Little Prince

Dahlia 'Old Gold'

Everything that slows us down and
forces patience, everything that
sets us back into the slow circles of
Nature, is a help. Gardening is an
instrument of grace.

MAY SARTON

Look about you. Take hold of the things
that are here. Let them talk to you.
You learn to talk to them.

GEORGE WASHINGTON CARVER

Rose
Rosa chinensis 'mutabilis'

In joy or sadness, flowers are our constant friends.

KAKUZŌ OKAKURA
The Book of Tea

One's delight in the garden depends . . . on the effects of sunlight and shadow, on massive bulk and relative emptiness contrasting with each other, on the effect of light on water, on the texture of brick and wood and stone.

HENRY MITCHELL
One Man's Garden

The highest reward for
a person's toil is not
what they get for it, but
what they become by it.

JOHN RUSKIN

In his garden every man may be his own
artist without apology or explanation.

LOUIS BEEBE WILDER

Nasturtium
Tropaeolum majus

Seaside Daisy
Erigeron glaucus

To own a bit of ground, to scratch
it with a hoe, to plant seeds, and
watch the renewal of life—this is the
commonest delight of the race, the
most satisfactory thing a man can do.

CHARLES DUDLEY WARNER

A garden is a grand teacher. It teaches
patience and careful watchfulness; it
teaches industry and thrift; above all
it teaches entire trust.

GERTRUDE JEKYLL

Gardens exist not only in the here and now, but in the there and then, too.

MICHAEL POLLAN
Second Nature

There are few gardens that can be left alone. A few years of neglect and only the skeleton of a garden can be traced.

RUSSELL PAGE
The Education of a Gardener

Hens and Chicks
Aeonium arboreum

Gardening is civil and social, but it wants the vigor and freedom of the forest and the outlaw.

HENRY DAVID THOREAU

Bearded Iris

Caring for another living entity is a basic
quality of being human. . . . In a world of
constant judgment, plants are non-threatening
and non-discriminating. . . . Plants take away
some of the anxiety and tension of the
immediate now by showing us that there are
long, enduring patterns in life.

CHARLES LEWIS

And the day came when the risk to remain tight in a bud was more painful than the risk it took to blossom.

ANAÏS NIN

Geranium
Pelargonium 'San Antonio'

If wildness can stop being (just) out there
and start being (also) in here, if it can start
being as humane as it is natural, then
perhaps we can get on with the unending task
of struggling to live rightly in the world—not
just in the garden, not just in the wilderness,
but in the home that encompasses them both.

WILLIAM CRONON
The Trouble with Wilderness

This used to be among my prayers—a piece of land not so very large, which would contain a garden . . .

HORACE
Satire

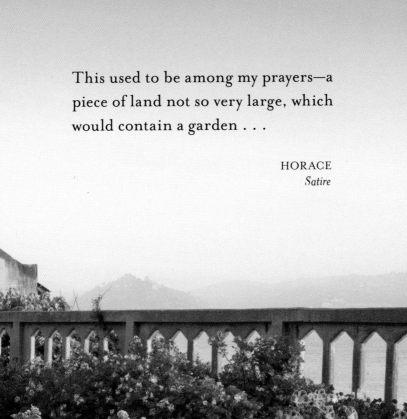

Man's heart away from nature
becomes hard.

CHIEF LUTHER STANDING BEAR
Oglala Sioux

One of the most important resources that a garden makes available for use is the gardener's own body. A garden gives the body the dignity of working in its own support. It is a way of rejoining the human race.

WENDELL BERRY

Mexican Evening Primrose
Oenothera speciosa

Flowers are restful to look at. They have neither emotions nor conflicts.

SIGMUND FREUD

Why stay we on the earth unless to grow?

ROBERT BROWNING
Cleon

A garden is a series of moments that somehow metamorphose into months and seasons and years.

JANICE EMILY BOWERS
A Full Life in a Small Place

I have a good job in the garden and greenhouse and have done so much hard work on them that I've grown a bit attached to the place.

RICHARD FRANZEEN
Inmate number AZ-387 (1937-1946)

Chasmanthe floribunda

Afterword

ABOUT THE PLANTS

No doubt the favorite plant on Alcatraz is also one of the most cherished of the ages, the **rose**, whose flower is the symbol of enduring love. Though individual varieties may seem delicate, the family includes some of the world's most resilient plants. On Alcatraz, we find cascading banks of rambling roses tumbling down the rocky slopes, climbers scrambling into trees and onto fences, and shrub roses used for hedging or for cut flowers.

- Ramblers and climbers: Russelliana, Dorothy Perkins, Excelsa, Félicité et Pérpetue, Blaze, Gardenia, Gloire des Rosomanes

- Early hybrid tea: General MacArthur

Rosa 'Russelliana'

Rosa 'Gruss an Achen'

Rosa 'General MacArthur'

Pelargoniums,
commonly referred to as
geraniums, are found in
many places on Alcatraz.
Their planting probably
dates to the army period,
both as garden plants in
the officers' gardens and
for beautification efforts
in the early 1900s.
Despite drought, wind,
and years of neglect,

Pelargonium 'Brilliant'

these plants are surprisingly healthy. The ease of
propagating pelargoniums from cuttings may help
explain their abundance on the island.

- Brilliant
- Prince Bismarck
- Alphonse Ricard
- San Antonio
- Mrs. Langtry

Long signature plants in California's coastal
gardens, **hybrid fuchsias** have endured the rigors of
Alcatraz surprisingly well.

- *Fuchsia magellanica*
- Mrs. Lovell Swisher
- Rose of Castile

Pelargonium 'San Antonio'

Fuchsia 'Rose of Castile'

Fuchsia 'Mrs. Lovell Swisher'

Bulbs and **bulblike plants** are eminently well-suited to Alcatraz's climate. In fact, many common bulbs originated in arid, Mediterranean-type regions, principally the Mediterranean Basin and South Africa. All of the plants from these regions found a home so similar to their natural habitat that they have naturalized on Alcatraz. The whole plant is literally a subterranean package that remains dormant during the summer and autumn. With winter rains, the dormant bulb springs to life, first producing leaves and later, spectacular bursts of flowers. Some bulbs expend their blooms in a few weeks, while others continue their show until the soil dries out. The straplike leaves of most bulbs function to catch any available moisture, even fog or dew, and funnel it to the bulb and its roots—an ingenious design for arid climates.

- Mediterranean Basin: *Hyacinthoides hispanica* (Spanish bluebell), *Leucojum aestivum* (summer snowflake), *Muscari armeniacum* (grape hyacinth), *Narcissus* (daffodil)

- South Africa: *Freesia, Amaryllis belladonna* (naked lady), *Chasmanthe, Watsonia, Homeria collina, Crocosmia x crocosmiiflora* (montbretia)

- California: Douglas iris, *Brodiaea*

Narcissus 'Barrett Browning'

Homeria collina

Crocosmia x *crocosmiiflora*

The island's gardens are a unique testing ground for **seaside plants.** Those that have endured have a number of traits in common, including origination in Mediterranean-type climatic regions; adaptation to cool summers and mild winters free of frost; toleration of strong, frequently salt-laden winds and fog and poor, rocky, or shallow soils; and the ability to thrive on winter rainfall and summer fog.

- Trees: *Cupressus macrocarpa* (Monterey cypress), *Eucalyptus globulus* (blue gum), *Leptospermum laevigatum*

Lily of the Nile

Valerian

Persian carpet

(Australian tea tree), *Metrosideros excelsa* (New Zealand Christmas tree)

- Shrubs: *Cistus* (rockrose), *Coprosma repens* (mirror plant), *Cotoneaster*, *Elaeagnus*, *Rhamnus californica* (coffeeberry), *Baccharis pilularis* (dwarf coyote brush)

- Succulents: *Aeonium arboreum* (hens and chicks), *Agave americana* (century plant), *Drosanthemum floribundum* (Persian carpet)

- Annuals: *Lobularia maritima* (sweet alyssum), *Eschscholzia californica* (California poppy), *Tropaeolum majus* (nasturtium)

- Perennials: *Centranthus ruber* (valerian), *Agapanthus orientalis* (Lily of the Nile), *Lathyrus latifolius* (sweet pea)

Because **fruit trees** usually demand more care and a warmer climate than is found on Alcatraz, it is surprising to see them here. But here they are. They were probably planted in the mid- to late 1930s, during the federal prison period.

· 3 apple trees, 2 plum trees, 2 walnut trees,
2 fig trees that have since naturalized

—RUSSELL A. BEATTY
Afterword adapted from "Long, Enduring Patterns,"
in *Gardens of Alcatraz*